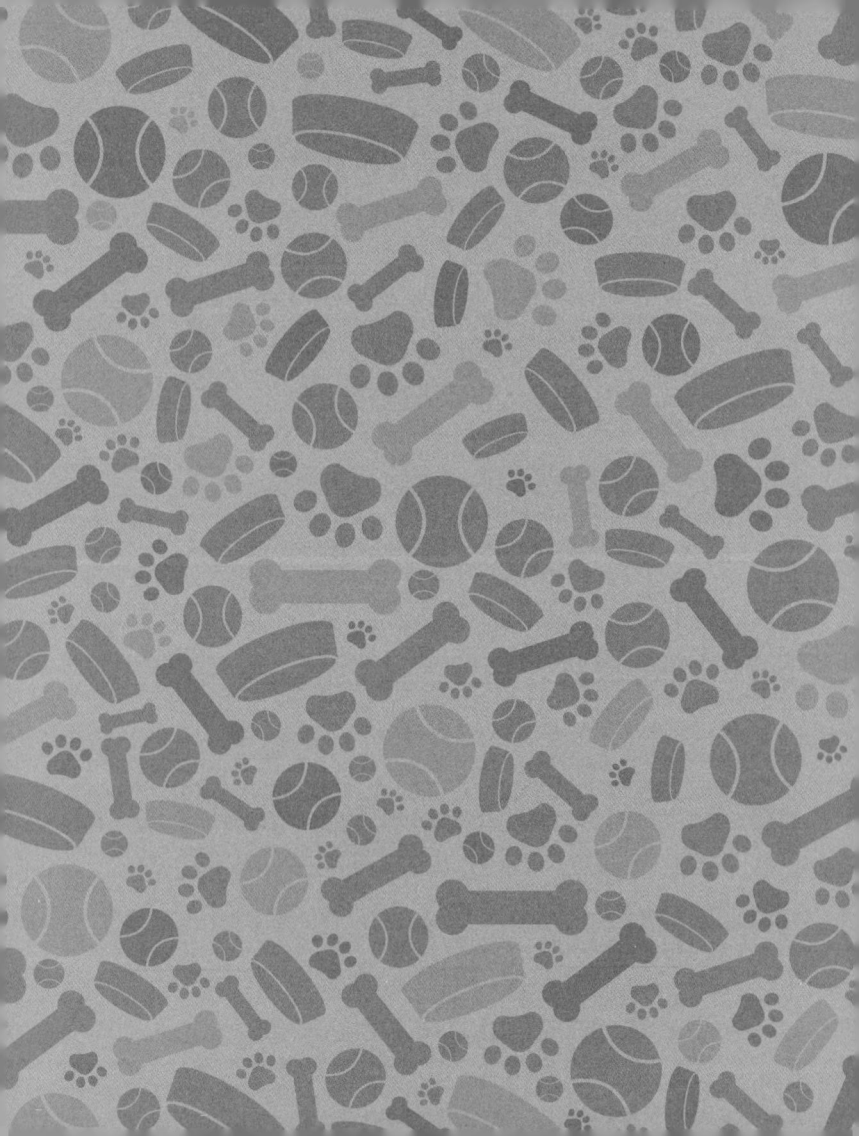

A JOURNAL

CHRONICLE BOOKS
SAN FRANCISCO

Copyright © 2012 by Chronicle Books LLC

All rights reserved. No part of this book may be reproduced in any form without written permission from the publisher.

ISBN: 978-1-4521-1196-4

Manufactured in China
Text by Steve Mockus
Designed by Kelsey Premo Jones

10 9 8 7 6 5 4 3 2 1

Chronicle Books LLC
680 Second Street
San Francisco, CA 94107

www.chroniclebooks.com

Chronicle Books publishes distinctive books and gifts. From award-winning children's titles, bestselling cookbooks, and eclectic pop culture to acclaimed works of art and design, stationery, and journals, we craft publishing that's instantly recognizable for its spirit and creativity. Enjoy our publishing and become part of our community at www.chroniclebooks.com.

Introduction

Some would have us believe that when a dog smiles, it is not really a "smile." They would tell us that when we trace the expression to the behavior of wolves, the deep ancestors of our dogs, the gesture of pulling back the corners of the mouth (smiling) is a sign of submission—in the case of a wolf pack, acceptance of the social order. But isn't contentment with social situations one of the most basic forms of happiness? Don't we smile when we're happy? Don't let anyone tell you otherwise: Your dog is definitely smiling.

There's a classic, unsigned viral humor item that compares the diaries of a cat and dog. An excerpt from the dog's:

> 8:00 A.M. — OH BOY! DOG FOOD! MY FAVORITE!
> 9:30 A.M. — OH BOY! A CAR RIDE! MY FAVORITE!
> 9:40 A.M. — OH BOY! A WALK! MY FAVORITE!

And that feels pretty close to the truth. Part of the fun of living with a dog is seeing how much they enjoy being a dog and being around us. We feel valued because they value us so highly.

It's now thought that dogs in part domesticated themselves, in that their ancestors saw the value of proximity to humans (tasty garbage) and hung around, first at a distance, until we each recognized the value of a belly rub and a scratch behind the ears. Our mutual appreciation and domestication progressed to the point that, although our dogs see us as the alpha dog, it's not always clear who's running the show. As Jerry Seinfeld point out, "If you see two life forms, one of them's making a poop, the other one's carrying it for him, who would you assume is in charge?"

We tend to personify our pets, especially our dogs, because we're so closely bonded, and we seem to see ourselves in each other. (Really, isn't the way a dog spends its walks peeing on certain things its own form of social networking, sniffing out other dogs' check-ins and leaving "status updates" of their own?)

Learning how dogs think makes us better caretakers and owners, by reading cues and providing them with what they need. This journal isn't so much about that important interaction, but about the lighter side of living with—in fact being—a dog. Your dog. Imagine: What are your goals for the day? What are you looking forward to the most? If you had thumbs, what would you do first?

In domestication, dogs and people started by essentially meeting each other halfway. Use this journal to get in touch with your dog mind, bond with your pet, have fun, and see the world through their eyes.

My dog's name: _____

Age: _____ ○ M ○ F Weight: _____ Eye color: _____

Fur color and markings: _____

Talents: _____

Tricks: _____

Hobbies: _____

Favorite toys: _____

Favorite toys that aren't toys: _____

Best friends: _____

Favorite foods: _____

Favorite treats: _____

Favorite smells: _____

Favorite walks: _____

Favorite napping spot: _____

If my dog had a job, it would be: _____

Celebrity my dog most resembles: _____

Three things you suspect that your dog does when you're not at home: _____

_____

_____

My dog is (check all that apply)

○ Regal

○ Goofy

○ Loyal

○ Friendly

○ Trusting

○ Cuddly

○ Insane

○ Sly

○ Adorable

○ Adventurous

○ Cautious

○ Independent

○ Brave

○ Active

○ Persistent

○ Lazy

○ Protective

○ Mellow

○ Proud

○ Quiet

○ Talkative

○ Funny

○ Smart

○ Opinionated

○ Sweet

○ Playful

○ Curious

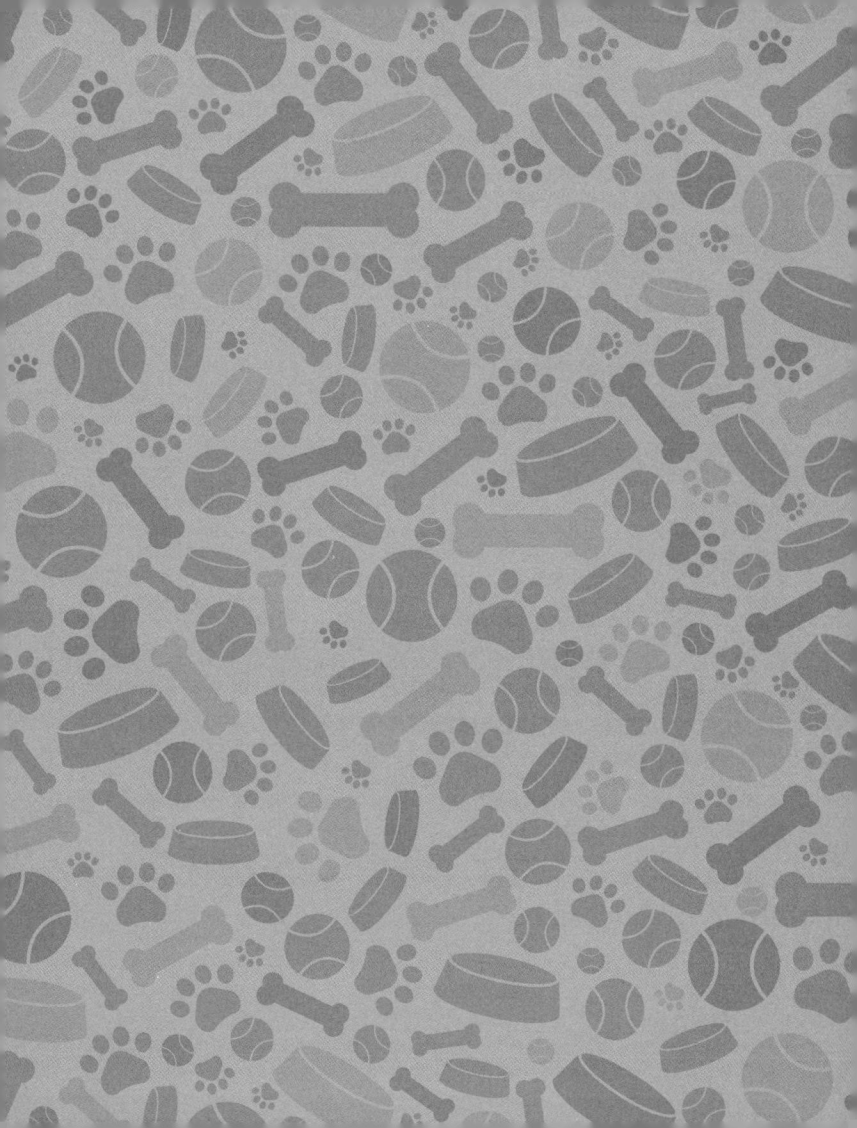

/ /

DATE

Goals for today: _____

_____

Notable achievements: _____

_____ Who's a good boy / girl? ◯ I am!

Cuteness scale

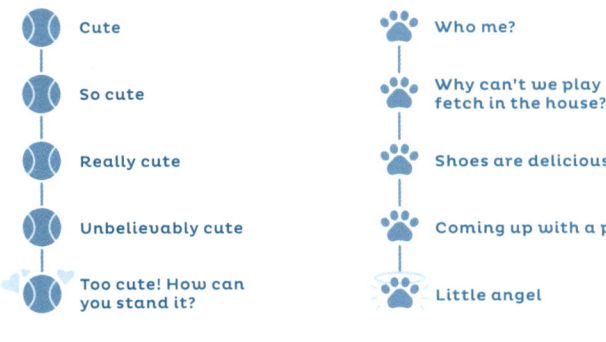

Cute

So cute

Really cute

Unbelievably cute

Too cute! How can you stand it?

Trouble scale

Who me?

Why can't we play fetch in the house?

Shoes are delicious

Coming up with a plan

Little angel

Cutest thing I did today: _____

_____

Trouble I got into: _____

_____

It was ◯ fun ◯ really fun

My walk(s)

Where: _____

What I saw / smelled: _____

Things I peed on: _____ Squirrel! ◯ Y ◯ N

Good things that happened today

- ○ Play catch
- ○ Chew toy
- ○ Car ride
- ○ Brushed
- ○ Belly rub
- ○ Scratch behind the ears
- ○ Nap

Food: _____

Treat: _____

Playtime: _____

Other: _____

If I had thumbs I would: _____

Lesson my owner learned from me today: _____

Thought for the day: _____

Draw what I am thinking right now:

If it wasn't for dogs, some people would never go for a walk.
—AUTHOR UNKNOWN

/ /

DATE

Goals for today: _____

_____

Notable achievements: _____

_____ Who's a good boy / girl? ○ I am!

Cuteness scale

Cute

So cute

Really cute

Unbelievably cute

Too cute! How can you stand it?

Trouble scale

Who me?

Why can't we play fetch in the house?

Shoes are delicious

Coming up with a plan

Little angel

Cutest thing I did today: _____

_____

Trouble I got into: _____

_____

It was ○ fun ○ really fun

My walk(s)

Where: _____

What I saw / smelled: _____

Things I peed on: _____ Squirrel! ○ Y ○ N

Good things that happened today

- ◯ Play catch
- ◯ Chew toy
- ◯ Car ride
- ◯ Brushed
- ◯ Belly rub
- ◯ Scratch behind the ears
- ◯ Nap

Food: _____

Treat: _____

Playtime: _____

Other: _____

If I had thumbs I would: _____

Lesson my owner learned from me today: _____

Thought for the day: _____

Draw what I am thinking right now:

There is no psychiatrist in the world like a puppy licking your face.
—BEN WILLIAMS

/ /

DATE

Goals for today: _____

_____

Notable achievements: _____

_____ Who's a good boy / girl? ◯ I am!

Cuteness scale

Cute

So cute

Really cute

Unbelievably cute

Too cute! How can you stand it?

Cutest thing I did today: _____

_____

Trouble scale

Who me?

Why can't we play fetch in the house?

Shoes are delicious

Coming up with a plan

Little angel

Trouble I got into: _____

_____

It was ◯ fun ◯ really fun

My walk(s)

Where: _____

What I saw / smelled: _____

Things I peed on: _____ Squirrel! ◯ Y ◯ N

Good things that happened today

- ◯ Play catch
- ◯ Chew toy
- ◯ Car ride
- ◯ Brushed
- ◯ Belly rub
- ◯ Scratch behind the ears
- ◯ Nap

Food: _____

Treat: _____

Playtime: _____

Other: _____

If I had thumbs I would: _____
_____
_____
_____

Lesson my owner learned from me today: _____
_____
_____
_____

Thought for the day: _____
_____
_____
_____

Draw what I am thinking right now:

Dogs are lousy poker players. When they get a good hand they wag their tails.
—AUTHOR UNKNOWN

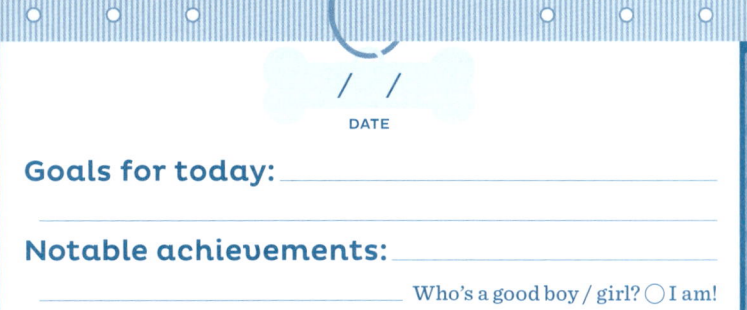

/ /

DATE

Goals for today: _____

_____

Notable achievements: _____

_____ Who's a good boy / girl? ◯ I am!

Cuteness scale

Cute

So cute

Really cute

Unbelievably cute

Too cute! How can you stand it?

Cutest thing I did today: _____

_____

My walk(s)

Where: _____

What I saw / smelled: _____

Things I peed on: _____

Trouble scale

Who me?

Why can't we play fetch in the house?

Shoes are delicious

Coming up with a plan

Little angel

Trouble I got into: _____

It was ◯ fun ◯ really fun

Squirrel! ◯ Y ◯ N

Good things that happened today

- ○ Play catch
- ○ Chew toy
- ○ Car ride
- ○ Brushed
- ○ Belly rub
- ○ Scratch behind the ears
- ○ Nap

Food: _____

Treat: _____

Playtime: _____

Other: _____

If I had thumbs I would: _____
_____
_____
_____

Lesson my owner learned from me today: _____
_____
_____
_____

Thought for the day: _____
_____
_____
_____

Draw what I am thinking right now:

Outside of a dog, a book is man's best friend. Inside a dog, it's too dark to read.
—GROUCHO MARX

/ /

DATE

Goals for today: _____

Notable achievements: _____

_____ Who's a good boy / girl? ◯ I am!

Cuteness scale

◯ Cute

◯ So cute

◯ Really cute

◯ Unbelievably cute

◯ Too cute! How can you stand it?

Cutest thing I did today: _____

_____

Trouble scale

Who me?

Why can't we play fetch in the house?

Shoes are delicious

Coming up with a plan

Little angel

Trouble I got into: _____

_____

It was ◯ fun ◯ really fun

My walk(s)

Where: _____

What I saw / smelled: _____

Things I peed on: _____ Squirrel! ◯ Y ◯ N

Good things that happened today

- ◯ Play catch
- ◯ Chew toy
- ◯ Car ride
- ◯ Brushed
- ◯ Belly rub
- ◯ Scratch behind the ears
- ◯ Nap

Food: _____

Treat: _____

Playtime: _____

Other: _____

If I had thumbs I would: _____
_____
_____
_____

Lesson my owner learned from me today: _____
_____
_____
_____

Thought for the day: _____
_____
_____
_____

Draw what I am thinking right now:

Dogs lead a nice life. You never see a dog with a wristwatch.
—GEORGE CARLIN

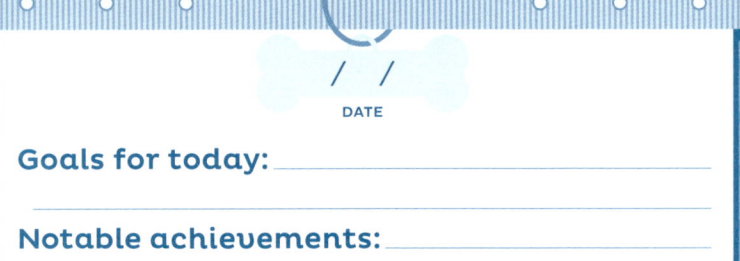

/ /

DATE

Goals for today: _____

_____

Notable achievements: _____

_____ Who's a good boy / girl? ◯ I am!

Cuteness scale

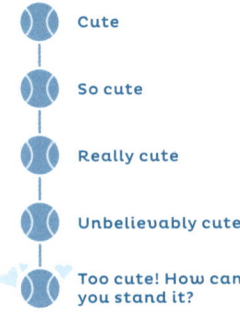

Cute

So cute

Really cute

Unbelievably cute

Too cute! How can you stand it?

Cutest thing I did today: _____

_____

Trouble scale

Who me?

Why can't we play fetch in the house?

Shoes are delicious

Coming up with a plan

Little angel

Trouble I got into: _____

_____

It was ◯ fun ◯ really fun

My walk(s)

Where: _____

What I saw / smelled: _____

Things I peed on: _____ Squirrel! ◯ Y ◯ N

Good things that happened today

- ◯ Play catch
- ◯ Chew toy
- ◯ Car ride
- ◯ Brushed
- ◯ Belly rub
- ◯ Scratch behind the ears
- ◯ Nap

Food: _____
Treat: _____
Playtime: _____
Other: _____

If I had thumbs I would: _____

Lesson my owner learned from me today: _____

Thought for the day: _____

Draw what I am thinking right now:

The great pleasure of a dog is that you may make a fool of yourself with him and not only will he not scold you, but he will make a fool of himself, too.
—SAMUEL BUTLER

/ /
DATE

Goals for today: _____
_____

Notable achievements: _____
_____ Who's a good boy / girl? ◯ I am!

Cuteness scale

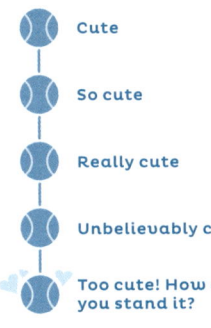

Cute

So cute

Really cute

Unbelievably cute

Too cute! How can you stand it?

Cutest thing I did today: _____
_____

Trouble scale

Who me?

Why can't we play fetch in the house?

Shoes are delicious

Coming up with a plan

Little angel

Trouble I got into: _____
_____

It was ◯ fun ◯ really fun

My walk(s)

Where: _____

What I saw / smelled: _____

Things I peed on: _____ Squirrel! ◯ Y ◯ N

Good things that happened today

- ◯ Play catch
- ◯ Chew toy
- ◯ Car ride
- ◯ Brushed
- ◯ Belly rub
- ◯ Scratch behind the ears
- ◯ Nap

Food: _____

Treat: _____

Playtime: _____

Other: _____

If I had thumbs I would: _____

_____

_____

_____

Lesson my owner learned from me today: _____

_____

_____

_____

Thought for the day: _____

_____

_____

_____

Draw what I am thinking right now:

Dogs are my favorite people.
—RICHARD DEAN ANDERSON

/ /

DATE

Goals for today: _____

_____

Notable achievements: _____

_____ Who's a good boy / girl? ◯ I am!

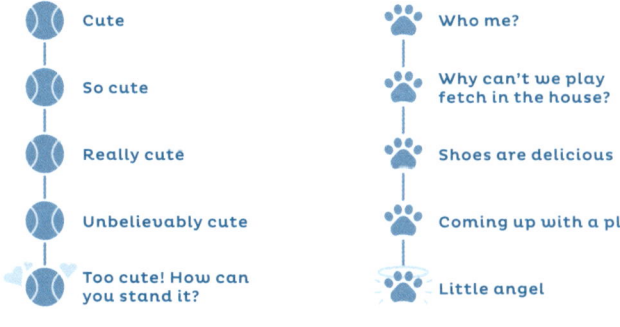

Cuteness scale

◯ Cute

◯ So cute

◯ Really cute

◯ Unbelievably cute

◯ Too cute! How can you stand it?

Cutest thing I did today: _____

_____

Trouble scale

Who me?

Why can't we play fetch in the house?

Shoes are delicious

Coming up with a plan

Little angel

Trouble I got into: _____

_____

It was ◯ fun ◯ really fun

My walk(s)

Where: _____

What I saw / smelled: _____

Things I peed on: _____ Squirrel! ◯ Y ◯ N

Good things that happened today

- ○ Play catch
- ○ Chew toy
- ○ Car ride
- ○ Brushed
- ○ Belly rub
- ○ Scratch behind the ears
- ○ Nap

Food: _____

Treat: _____

Playtime: _____

Other: _____

If I had thumbs I would: _____

Lesson my owner learned from me today: _____

Thought for the day: _____

Draw what I am thinking right now:

A dog is the only thing on earth that loves you more than he loves himself.
—JOSH BILLINGS

/ /
DATE

Goals for today: _____

_____

Notable achievements: _____

_____ Who's a good boy / girl? ○ I am!

Cuteness scale

● Cute

● So cute

● Really cute

● Unbelievably cute

● Too cute! How can you stand it?

Cutest thing I did today: _____

_____

Trouble scale

🐾 Who me?

🐾 Why can't we play fetch in the house?

🐾 Shoes are delicious

🐾 Coming up with a plan

🐾 Little angel

Trouble I got into: _____

_____

It was ○ fun ○ really fun

My walk(s)

Where: _____

What I saw / smelled: _____

Things I peed on: _____ Squirrel! ○ Y ○ N

Good things that happened today

- ◯ Play catch
- ◯ Chew toy
- ◯ Car ride
- ◯ Brushed
- ◯ Belly rub
- ◯ Scratch behind the ears
- ◯ Nap

Food: _____
Treat: _____
Playtime: _____
Other: _____

Draw what I am thinking right now:

If I had thumbs I would: _____

Lesson my owner learned from me today: _____

Thought for the day: _____

If it wasn't for dogs, some people would never go for a walk.
—AUTHOR UNKNOWN

/ /

DATE

Goals for today: _____

_____

Notable achievements: _____

_____ Who's a good boy / girl? ◯ I am!

Cuteness scale

Cute

So cute

Really cute

Unbelievably cute

Too cute! How can you stand it?

Trouble scale

Who me?

Why can't we play fetch in the house?

Shoes are delicious

Coming up with a plan

Little angel

Cutest thing I did today: _____

_____

Trouble I got into: _____

It was ◯ fun ◯ really fun

My walk(s)

Where: _____

What I saw / smelled: _____

Things I peed on: _____ Squirrel! ◯ Y ◯ N

Good things that happened today

- ◯ Play catch
- ◯ Chew toy
- ◯ Car ride
- ◯ Brushed
- ◯ Belly rub
- ◯ Scratch behind the ears
- ◯ Nap

Food: _____

Treat: _____

Playtime: _____

Other: _____

If I had thumbs I would: _____

Lesson my owner learned from me today: _____

Thought for the day: _____

Draw what I am thinking right now:

There is no psychiatrist in the world like a puppy licking your face.
—BEN WILLIAMS

/ /
DATE

Goals for today: _____

_____

Notable achievements: _____

_____ Who's a good boy / girl? ◯ I am!

Cuteness scale

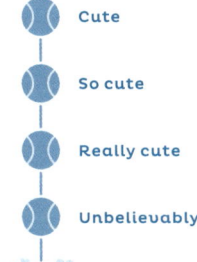

Cute

So cute

Really cute

Unbelievably cute

Too cute! How can you stand it?

Cutest thing I did today: _____

_____

Trouble scale

Who me?

Why can't we play fetch in the house?

Shoes are delicious

Coming up with a plan

Little angel

Trouble I got into: _____

It was ◯ fun ◯ really fun

My walk(s)

Where: _____

What I saw / smelled: _____

Things I peed on: _____ Squirrel! ◯ Y ◯ N

Good things that happened today

- ○ Play catch
- ○ Chew toy
- ○ Car ride
- ○ Brushed
- ○ Belly rub
- ○ Scratch behind the ears
- ○ Nap

Food: _____

Treat: _____

Playtime: _____

Other: _____

If I had thumbs I would: _____

Lesson my owner learned from me today: _____

Thought for the day: _____

Draw what I am thinking right now:

Dogs are lousy poker players. When they get a good hand they wag their tails.

—AUTHOR UNKNOWN

/ /
DATE

Goals for today: _____

_____

Notable achievements: _____

_____ Who's a good boy / girl? ○ I am!

Cuteness scale

● Cute

● So cute

● Really cute

● Unbelievably cute

● Too cute! How can you stand it?

Cutest thing I did today: _____

_____

My walk(s)

Where: _____

What I saw / smelled: _____

Things I peed on: _____

Trouble scale

🐾 Who me?

🐾 Why can't we play fetch in the house?

🐾 Shoes are delicious

🐾 Coming up with a plan

🐾 Little angel

Trouble I got into: _____

_____

It was ○ fun ○ really fun

Squirrel! ○ Y ○ N

Good things that happened today

- ○ Play catch
- ○ Chew toy
- ○ Car ride
- ○ Brushed
- ○ Belly rub
- ○ Scratch behind the ears
- ○ Nap

Food: _____

Treat: _____

Playtime: _____

Other: _____

If I had thumbs I would: _____

Lesson my owner learned from me today: _____

Thought for the day: _____

Draw what I am thinking right now:

Outside of a dog, a book is man's best friend. Inside a dog, it's too dark to read.
—GROUCHO MARX

/ /

DATE

Goals for today: _____

_____

Notable achievements: _____

_____ Who's a good boy / girl? ◯ I am!

Cuteness scale

Cute

So cute

Really cute

Unbelievably cute

Too cute! How can you stand it?

Trouble scale

Who me?

Why can't we play fetch in the house?

Shoes are delicious

Coming up with a plan

Little angel

Cutest thing I did today: _____

_____

Trouble I got into: _____

_____

It was ◯ fun ◯ really fun

My walk(s)

Where: _____

What I saw / smelled: _____

Things I peed on: _____ Squirrel! ◯ Y ◯ N

Good things that happened today

- ○ Play catch
- ○ Chew toy
- ○ Car ride
- ○ Brushed
- ○ Belly rub
- ○ Scratch behind the ears
- ○ Nap

Food: _____

Treat: _____

Playtime: _____

Other: _____

If I had thumbs I would: _____

Lesson my owner learned from me today: _____

Thought for the day: _____

Draw what I am thinking right now:

Dogs lead a nice life. You never see a dog with a wristwatch.
—GEORGE CARLIN

/ /
DATE

Goals for today: _____

_____

Notable achievements: _____

_____ Who's a good boy / girl? ◯ I am!

Cuteness scale

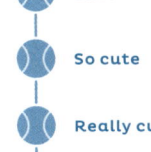 Cute

So cute

Really cute

Unbelievably cute

Too cute! How can
you stand it?

Trouble scale

 Who me?

Why can't we play
fetch in the house?

Shoes are delicious

Coming up with a plan

Little angel

Cutest thing I did today: _____

_____

Trouble I got into: _____

It was ◯ fun ◯ really fun

My walk(s)

Where: _____

What I saw / smelled: _____

Things I peed on: _____ Squirrel! ◯ Y ◯ N

Good things that happened today

- ◯ Play catch
- ◯ Chew toy
- ◯ Car ride
- ◯ Brushed
- ◯ Belly rub
- ◯ Scratch behind the ears
- ◯ Nap

Food: _____

Treat: _____

Playtime: _____

Other: _____

If I had thumbs I would: _____

Lesson my owner learned from me today: _____

Thought for the day: _____

Draw what I am thinking right now:

The great pleasure of a dog is that you may make a fool of yourself with him and not only will he not scold you, but he will make a fool of himself, too.
—SAMUEL BUTLER

/ /

DATE

Goals for today: _____

_____

Notable achievements: _____

_____ Who's a good boy / girl? ○ I am!

Cuteness scale

Cute

So cute

Really cute

Unbelievably cute

Too cute! How can you stand it?

Trouble scale

Who me?

Why can't we play fetch in the house?

Shoes are delicious

Coming up with a plan

Little angel

Cutest thing I did today: _____

_____

My walk(s)

Trouble I got into: _____

_____

It was ○ fun ○ really fun

Where: _____

What I saw / smelled: _____

Things I peed on: _____ Squirrel! ○ Y ○ N

Good things that happened today

- ◯ Play catch
- ◯ Chew toy
- ◯ Car ride
- ◯ Brushed
- ◯ Belly rub
- ◯ Scratch behind the ears
- ◯ Nap

Food: _____

Treat: _____

Playtime: _____

Other: _____

If I had thumbs I would: _____
_____
_____
_____

Lesson my owner learned from me today: _____
_____
_____
_____

Thought for the day: _____
_____
_____
_____

Draw what I am thinking right now:

Dogs are my favorite people.
—RICHARD DEAN ANDERSON

/ /

DATE

Goals for today: _____

_____

Notable achievements: _____

_____ Who's a good boy / girl? ◯ I am!

Cuteness scale

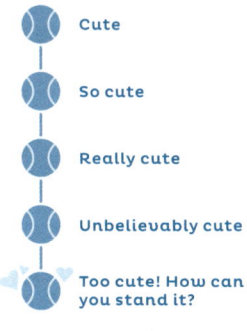

Cute

So cute

Really cute

Unbelievably cute

Too cute! How can you stand it?

Trouble scale

Who me?

Why can't we play fetch in the house?

Shoes are delicious

Coming up with a plan

Little angel

Cutest thing I did today: _____

_____

Trouble I got into: _____

_____

It was ◯ fun ◯ really fun

My walk(s)

Where: _____

What I saw / smelled: _____

Things I peed on: _____ Squirrel! ◯ Y ◯ N

Good things that happened today

- ◯ Play catch
- ◯ Chew toy
- ◯ Car ride
- ◯ Brushed
- ◯ Belly rub
- ◯ Scratch behind the ears
- ◯ Nap

Food: _____

Treat: _____

Playtime: _____

Other: _____

If I had thumbs I would: _____

Lesson my owner learned from me today: _____

Thought for the day: _____

Draw what I am thinking right now:

A dog is the only thing on earth that loves you more than he loves himself.
—JOSH BILLINGS

/ /
DATE

Goals for today: _____

_____

Notable achievements: _____

_____ Who's a good boy / girl? ◯ I am!

Cuteness scale

Cute

So cute

Really cute

Unbelievably cute

Too cute! How can you stand it?

Cutest thing I did today: _____

_____

Trouble scale

Who me?

Why can't we play fetch in the house?

Shoes are delicious

Coming up with a plan

Little angel

Trouble I got into: _____

_____

It was ◯ fun ◯ really fun

My walk(s)

Where: _____

What I saw / smelled: _____

Things I peed on: _____ Squirrel! ◯ Y ◯ N

Good things that happened today

- ○ Play catch
- ○ Chew toy
- ○ Car ride
- ○ Brushed
- ○ Belly rub
- ○ Scratch behind the ears
- ○ Nap

Food: _____

Treat: _____

Playtime: _____

Other: _____

If I had thumbs I would: _____

Lesson my owner learned from me today: _____

Thought for the day: _____

Draw what I am thinking right now:

If it wasn't for dogs, some people would never go for a walk.
—AUTHOR UNKNOWN

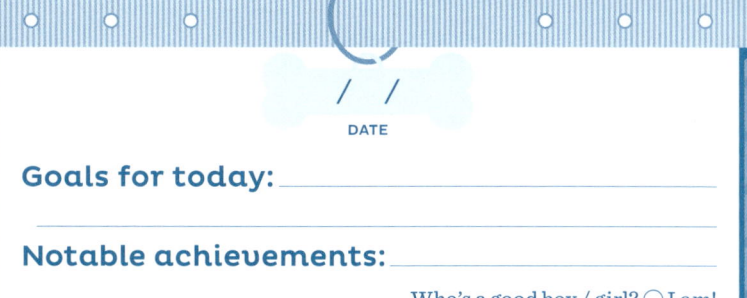

/ /

DATE

Goals for today: _____

_____

Notable achievements: _____

_____ Who's a good boy / girl? ○ I am!

Cuteness scale

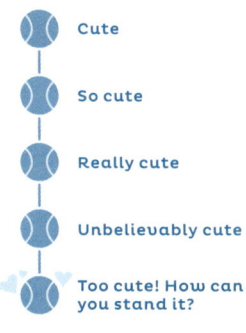

Cute

So cute

Really cute

Unbelievably cute

Too cute! How can
you stand it?

Cutest thing I did today: _____

_____

Trouble scale

Who me?

Why can't we play
fetch in the house?

Shoes are delicious

Coming up with a plan

Little angel

Trouble I got into: _____

_____

It was ○ fun ○ really fun

My walk(s)

Where: _____

What I saw / smelled: _____

Things I peed on: _____ Squirrel! ○ Y ○ N

Good things that happened today

- ○ Play catch
- ○ Chew toy
- ○ Car ride
- ○ Brushed
- ○ Belly rub
- ○ Scratch behind the ears
- ○ Nap

Food: _____

Treat: _____

Playtime: _____

Other: _____

If I had thumbs I would: _____

Lesson my owner learned from me today: _____

Thought for the day: _____

Draw what I am thinking right now:

There is no psychiatrist in the world like a puppy licking your face.
—BEN WILLIAMS

DATE

Goals for today: _____
_____

Notable achievements: _____
_____ Who's a good boy / girl? ○ I am!

Cuteness scale

Cute

So cute

Really cute

Unbelievably cute

Too cute! How can you stand it?

Cutest thing I did today: _____
_____

Trouble scale

Who me?

Why can't we play fetch in the house?

Shoes are delicious

Coming up with a plan

Little angel

Trouble I got into: _____

It was ○ fun ○ really fun

My walk(s)

Where: _____

What I saw / smelled: _____

Things I peed on: _____ Squirrel! ○ Y ○ N

Good things that happened today

- ◯ Play catch
- ◯ Chew toy
- ◯ Car ride
- ◯ Brushed
- ◯ Belly rub
- ◯ Scratch behind the ears
- ◯ Nap

Food: _____

Treat: _____

Playtime: _____

Other: _____

If I had thumbs I would: _____

Lesson my owner learned from me today: _____

Thought for the day: _____

Draw what I am thinking right now:

Dogs are lousy poker players. When they get a good hand they wag their tails.

—AUTHOR UNKNOWN

/ /
DATE

Goals for today: _____

_____

Notable achievements: _____

_____ Who's a good boy / girl? ◯ I am!

Cuteness scale

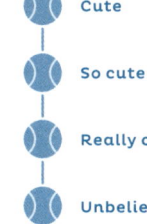

Cute

So cute

Really cute

Unbelievably cute

Too cute! How can you stand it?

Trouble scale

Who me?

Why can't we play fetch in the house?

Shoes are delicious

Coming up with a plan

Little angel

Cutest thing I did today: _____

_____

Trouble I got into: _____

It was ◯ fun ◯ really fun

My walk(s)

Where: _____

What I saw / smelled: _____

Things I peed on: _____ Squirrel! ◯ Y ◯ N

Good things that happened today

- ◯ Play catch
- ◯ Chew toy
- ◯ Car ride
- ◯ Brushed
- ◯ Belly rub
- ◯ Scratch behind the ears
- ◯ Nap

Food: _____

Treat: _____

Playtime: _____

Other: _____

If I had thumbs I would: _____

Lesson my owner learned from me today: _____

Thought for the day: _____

Draw what I am thinking right now:

Outside of a dog, a book is man's best friend. Inside a dog, it's too dark to read.

—GROUCHO MARX

DATE / /

Goals for today: _____

_____

Notable achievements: _____

_____ Who's a good boy / girl? ◯ I am!

Cuteness scale

Cute

So cute

Really cute

Unbelievably cute

Too cute! How can you stand it?

Trouble scale

Who me?

Why can't we play fetch in the house?

Shoes are delicious

Coming up with a plan

Little angel

Cutest thing I did today: _____

_____

Trouble I got into: _____

_____

It was ◯ fun ◯ really fun

My walk(s)

Where: _____

What I saw / smelled: _____

Things I peed on: _____ Squirrel! ◯ Y ◯ N

Good things that happened today

- ○ Play catch
- ○ Chew toy
- ○ Car ride
- ○ Brushed
- ○ Belly rub
- ○ Scratch behind the ears
- ○ Nap

Food: _____

Treat: _____

Playtime: _____

Other: _____

If I had thumbs I would: _____

Lesson my owner learned from me today: _____

Thought for the day: _____

Draw what I am thinking right now:

Dogs lead a nice life. You never see a dog with a wristwatch.
—GEORGE CARLIN

/ /

DATE

Goals for today: _____

_____

Notable achievements: _____

_____ Who's a good boy / girl? ○ I am!

Cuteness scale

- 🎾 Cute
- 🎾 So cute
- 🎾 Really cute
- 🎾 Unbelievably cute
- 🎾 Too cute! How can you stand it?

Cutest thing I did today: _____

_____

My walk(s)

Where: _____

What I saw / smelled: _____

Things I peed on: _____

Trouble scale

- 🐾 Who me?
- 🐾 Why can't we play fetch in the house?
- 🐾 Shoes are delicious
- 🐾 Coming up with a plan
- 🐾 Little angel

Trouble I got into: _____

_____

It was ○ fun ○ really fun

Squirrel! ○ Y ○ N

Good things that happened today

- ○ Play catch
- ○ Chew toy
- ○ Car ride
- ○ Brushed
- ○ Belly rub
- ○ Scratch behind the ears
- ○ Nap

Food: _____

Treat: _____

Playtime: _____

Other: _____

If I had thumbs I would: _____
_____
_____
_____

Lesson my owner learned from me today: _____
_____
_____
_____

Thought for the day: _____
_____
_____
_____

Draw what I am thinking right now:

The great pleasure of a dog is that you may make a fool of yourself with him and not only will he not scold you, but he will make a fool of himself, too.
—SAMUEL BUTLER

/ /

DATE

Goals for today: _____

_____

Notable achievements: _____

_____ Who's a good boy / girl? ○ I am!

Cuteness scale

Cute

So cute

Really cute

Unbelievably cute

Too cute! How can you stand it?

Cutest thing I did today: _____

_____

Trouble scale

Who me?

Why can't we play fetch in the house?

Shoes are delicious

Coming up with a plan

Little angel

Trouble I got into: _____

_____

It was ○ fun ○ really fun

My walk(s)

Where: _____

What I saw / smelled: _____

Things I peed on: _____ Squirrel! ○ Y ○ N

Good things that happened today

- ◯ Play catch
- ◯ Chew toy
- ◯ Car ride
- ◯ Brushed
- ◯ Belly rub
- ◯ Scratch behind the ears
- ◯ Nap

Food: _____

Treat: _____

Playtime: _____

Other: _____

If I had thumbs I would: _____

Lesson my owner learned from me today: _____

Thought for the day: _____

Draw what I am thinking right now:

Dogs are my favorite people.
—RICHARD DEAN ANDERSON

DATE / /

Goals for today: _____

_____

Notable achievements: _____

_____ Who's a good boy / girl? ○ I am!

Cuteness scale

○ Cute

○ So cute

○ Really cute

○ Unbelievably cute

○ Too cute! How can you stand it?

Cutest thing I did today: _____

_____

Trouble scale

○ Who me?

○ Why can't we play fetch in the house?

○ Shoes are delicious

○ Coming up with a plan

○ Little angel

Trouble I got into: _____

_____

It was ○ fun ○ really fun

My walk(s)

Where: _____

What I saw / smelled: _____

Things I peed on: _____ Squirrel! ○ Y ○ N

Good things that happened today

- ◯ Play catch
- ◯ Chew toy
- ◯ Car ride
- ◯ Brushed
- ◯ Belly rub
- ◯ Scratch behind the ears
- ◯ Nap

Food: _____

Treat: _____

Playtime: _____

Other: _____

If I had thumbs I would: _____

Lesson my owner learned from me today: _____

Thought for the day: _____

Draw what I am thinking right now:

A dog is the only thing on earth that loves you more than he loves himself.
—JOSH BILLINGS

/ /
DATE

Goals for today: _____
_____

Notable achievements: _____
_____ Who's a good boy / girl? ◯ I am!

Cuteness scale

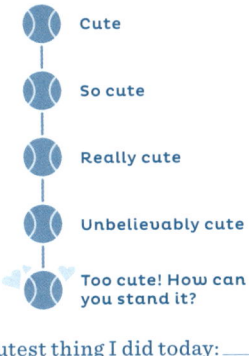

Cute

So cute

Really cute

Unbelievably cute

Too cute! How can you stand it?

Cutest thing I did today: _____
_____

Trouble scale

Who me?

Why can't we play fetch in the house?

Shoes are delicious

Coming up with a plan

Little angel

Trouble I got into: _____
_____

It was ◯ fun ◯ really fun

My walk(s)

Where: _____

What I saw / smelled: _____

Things I peed on: _____ Squirrel! ◯ Y ◯ N

Good things that happened today

- ○ Play catch
- ○ Chew toy
- ○ Car ride
- ○ Brushed
- ○ Belly rub
- ○ Scratch behind the ears
- ○ Nap

Food: _____

Treat: _____

Playtime: _____

Other: _____

If I had thumbs I would: _____

Lesson my owner learned from me today: _____

Thought for the day: _____

Draw what I am thinking right now:

If it wasn't for dogs, some people would never go for a walk.
—AUTHOR UNKNOWN

/ /
DATE

Goals for today: _____

_____

Notable achievements: _____

_____ Who's a good boy / girl? ◯ I am!

Cuteness scale

🎾 Cute

🎾 So cute

🎾 Really cute

🎾 Unbelievably cute

🎾 Too cute! How can you stand it?

Cutest thing I did today: _____

_____

Trouble scale

🐾 Who me?

🐾 Why can't we play fetch in the house?

🐾 Shoes are delicious

🐾 Coming up with a plan

🐾 Little angel

Trouble I got into: _____

_____

It was ◯ fun ◯ really fun

My walk(s)

Where: _____

What I saw / smelled: _____

Things I peed on: _____ Squirrel! ◯ Y ◯ N

Good things that happened today

- ○ Play catch
- ○ Chew toy
- ○ Car ride
- ○ Brushed
- ○ Belly rub
- ○ Scratch behind the ears
- ○ Nap

Food: _____

Treat: _____

Playtime: _____

Other: _____

If I had thumbs I would: _____

Lesson my owner learned from me today: _____

Thought for the day: _____

Draw what I am thinking right now:

There is no psychiatrist in the world like a puppy licking your face.
—BEN WILLIAMS

/ /
DATE

Goals for today: _____
_____

Notable achievements: _____
_____ Who's a good boy / girl? ◯ I am!

Cuteness scale

🎾 Cute

🎾 So cute

🎾 Really cute

🎾 Unbelievably cute

🎾 Too cute! How can you stand it?

Cutest thing I did today: _____
_____

Trouble scale

🐾 Who me?

🐾 Why can't we play fetch in the house?

🐾 Shoes are delicious

🐾 Coming up with a plan

🐾 Little angel

Trouble I got into: _____
_____

It was ◯ fun ◯ really fun

My walk(s)

Where: _____

What I saw / smelled: _____

Things I peed on: _____ Squirrel! ◯ Y ◯ N

Good things that happened today

- ◯ Play catch
- ◯ Chew toy
- ◯ Car ride
- ◯ Brushed
- ◯ Belly rub
- ◯ Scratch behind the ears
- ◯ Nap

Food: _____

Treat: _____

Playtime: _____

Other: _____

If I had thumbs I would: _____

Lesson my owner learned from me today: _____

Thought for the day: _____

Draw what I am thinking right now:

Dogs are lousy poker players. When they get a good hand they wag their tails.
—AUTHOR UNKNOWN

/ /
DATE

Goals for today: _____

_____

Notable achievements: _____

_____ Who's a good boy / girl? ◯ I am!

Cuteness scale

🎾 Cute

🎾 So cute

🎾 Really cute

🎾 Unbelievably cute

🎾 Too cute! How can you stand it?

Cutest thing I did today: _____

_____

Trouble scale

🐾 Who me?

🐾 Why can't we play fetch in the house?

🐾 Shoes are delicious

🐾 Coming up with a plan

🐾 Little angel

Trouble I got into: _____

It was ◯ fun ◯ really fun

My walk(s)

Where: _____

What I saw / smelled: _____

Things I peed on: _____ Squirrel! ◯ Y ◯ N

Good things that happened today

- ◯ Play catch
- ◯ Chew toy
- ◯ Car ride
- ◯ Brushed
- ◯ Belly rub
- ◯ Scratch behind the ears
- ◯ Nap

Food: _____

Treat: _____

Playtime: _____

Other: _____

If I had thumbs I would: _____
_____
_____
_____

Lesson my owner learned from me today: _____
_____
_____
_____

Thought for the day: _____
_____
_____
_____

Draw what I am thinking right now:

Outside of a dog, a book is man's best friend. Inside a dog, it's too dark to read.
—GROUCHO MARX

/ /
DATE

Goals for today: _____

_____

Notable achievements: _____

_____ Who's a good boy / girl? ◯ I am!

Cuteness scale

○ Cute

○ So cute

○ Really cute

○ Unbelievably cute

○ Too cute! How can you stand it?

Cutest thing I did today: _____

_____

Trouble scale

🐾 Who me?

🐾 Why can't we play fetch in the house?

🐾 Shoes are delicious

🐾 Coming up with a plan

🐾 Little angel

Trouble I got into: _____

It was ◯ fun ◯ really fun

My walk(s)

Where: _____

What I saw / smelled: _____

Things I peed on: _____ Squirrel! ◯ Y ◯ N

Good things that happened today

- ◯ Play catch
- ◯ Chew toy
- ◯ Car ride
- ◯ Brushed
- ◯ Belly rub
- ◯ Scratch behind the ears
- ◯ Nap

Food: _____

Treat: _____

Playtime: _____

Other: _____

Draw what I am thinking right now:

If I had thumbs I would: _____
_____
_____
_____

Lesson my owner learned from me today: _____
_____
_____
_____

Thought for the day: _____
_____
_____
_____

Dogs lead a nice life. You never see a dog with a wristwatch.
—GEORGE CARLIN

/ /

DATE

Goals for today: _____

_____

Notable achievements: _____

_____ Who's a good boy / girl? ○ I am!

Cuteness scale

🎾 Cute

🎾 So cute

🎾 Really cute

🎾 Unbelievably cute

🎾 Too cute! How can you stand it?

Cutest thing I did today: _____

_____

Trouble scale

🐾 Who me?

🐾 Why can't we play fetch in the house?

🐾 Shoes are delicious

🐾 Coming up with a plan

🐾 Little angel

Trouble I got into: _____

_____

It was ○ fun ○ really fun

My walk(s)

Where: _____

What I saw / smelled: _____

Things I peed on: _____ Squirrel! ○ Y ○ N

Good things that happened today

- ◯ Play catch
- ◯ Chew toy
- ◯ Car ride
- ◯ Brushed
- ◯ Belly rub
- ◯ Scratch behind the ears
- ◯ Nap

Food: _____

Treat: _____

Playtime: _____

Other: _____

If I had thumbs I would: _____

Lesson my owner learned from me today: _____

Thought for the day: _____

Draw what I am thinking right now:

The great pleasure of a dog is that you may make a fool of yourself with him and not only will he not scold you, but he will make a fool of himself, too.

—SAMUEL BUTLER

/ /
DATE

Goals for today: _____

_____

Notable achievements: _____

_____ Who's a good boy / girl? ○ I am!

Cuteness scale

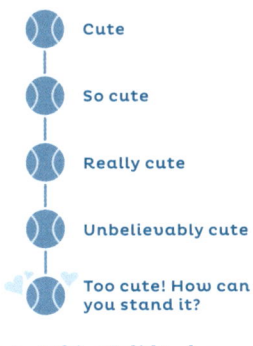

Cute

So cute

Really cute

Unbelievably cute

Too cute! How can you stand it?

Cutest thing I did today: _____

_____

Trouble scale

Who me?

Why can't we play fetch in the house?

Shoes are delicious

Coming up with a plan

Little angel

Trouble I got into: _____

_____

It was ○ fun ○ really fun

My walk(s)

Where: _____

What I saw / smelled: _____

Things I peed on: _____ Squirrel! ○ Y ○ N

Good things that happened today

- ◯ Play catch
- ◯ Chew toy
- ◯ Car ride
- ◯ Brushed
- ◯ Belly rub
- ◯ Scratch behind the ears
- ◯ Nap

Food: _____

Treat: _____

Playtime: _____

Other: _____

If I had thumbs I would: _____

Lesson my owner learned from me today: _____

Thought for the day: _____

Draw what I am thinking right now:

Dogs are my favorite people.
—RICHARD DEAN ANDERSON

/ / /
DATE

Goals for today: _____

_____

Notable achievements: _____

_____ Who's a good boy / girl? ◯ I am!

Cuteness scale

Cute

So cute

Really cute

Unbelievably cute

Too cute! How can you stand it?

Cutest thing I did today: _____

_____

My walk(s)

Trouble scale

Who me?

Why can't we play fetch in the house?

Shoes are delicious

Coming up with a plan

Little angel

Trouble I got into: _____

_____

It was ◯ fun ◯ really fun

Where: _____

What I saw / smelled: _____

Things I peed on: _____ Squirrel! ◯ Y ◯ N

Good things that happened today

- ◯ Play catch
- ◯ Chew toy
- ◯ Car ride
- ◯ Brushed
- ◯ Belly rub
- ◯ Scratch behind the ears
- ◯ Nap

Food: _____

Treat: _____

Playtime: _____

Other: _____

If I had thumbs I would: _____
_____
_____
_____

Lesson my owner learned from me today: _____
_____
_____
_____

Thought for the day: _____
_____
_____
_____

Draw what I am thinking right now:

A dog is the only thing on earth that loves you more than he loves himself.
—JOSH BILLINGS

/ /

DATE

Goals for today: _____

_____

Notable achievements: _____

_____ Who's a good boy / girl? ◯ I am!

Cuteness scale

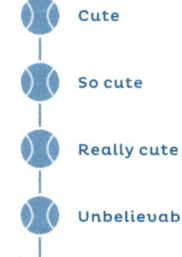

Cute

So cute

Really cute

Unbelievably cute

Too cute! How can you stand it?

Cutest thing I did today: _____

_____

Trouble scale

Who me?

Why can't we play fetch in the house?

Shoes are delicious

Coming up with a plan

Little angel

Trouble I got into: _____

_____

It was ◯ fun ◯ really fun

My walk(s)

Where: _____

What I saw / smelled: _____

Things I peed on: _____ Squirrel! ◯ Y ◯ N

Good things that happened today

- ◯ Play catch
- ◯ Chew toy
- ◯ Car ride
- ◯ Brushed
- ◯ Belly rub
- ◯ Scratch behind the ears
- ◯ Nap

Food: _____

Treat: _____

Playtime: _____

Other: _____

If I had thumbs I would: _____
_____
_____
_____

Lesson my owner learned from me today: _____
_____
_____
_____

Thought for the day: _____
_____
_____
_____

Draw what I am thinking right now:

If it wasn't for dogs, some people would never go for a walk.
—AUTHOR UNKNOWN

DATE

Goals for today: _____

_____

Notable achievements: _____

_____ Who's a good boy / girl? ○ I am!

Cuteness scale

Cute

So cute

Really cute

Unbelievably cute

Too cute! How can you stand it?

Cutest thing I did today: _____

_____

Trouble scale

Who me?

Why can't we play fetch in the house?

Shoes are delicious

Coming up with a plan

Little angel

Trouble I got into: _____

_____

It was ○ fun ○ really fun

My walk(s)

Where: _____

What I saw / smelled: _____

Things I peed on: _____ Squirrel! ○ Y ○ N

Good things that happened today

- ◯ Play catch
- ◯ Chew toy
- ◯ Car ride
- ◯ Brushed
- ◯ Belly rub
- ◯ Scratch behind the ears
- ◯ Nap

Food: _____

Treat: _____

Playtime: _____

Other: _____

If I had thumbs I would: _____
_____
_____
_____

Lesson my owner learned from me today: _____
_____
_____
_____

Thought for the day: _____
_____
_____
_____

Draw what I am thinking right now:

There is no psychiatrist in the world like a puppy licking your face.
—BEN WILLIAMS

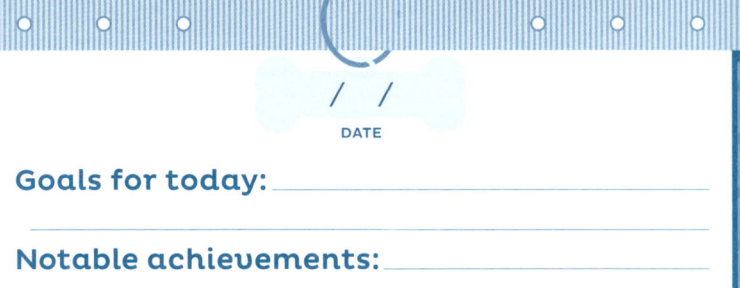

DATE / /

Goals for today: _____

_____

Notable achievements: _____

_____ Who's a good boy / girl? ◯ I am!

Cuteness scale

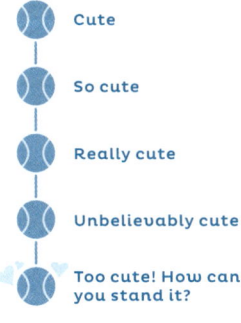

Cute

So cute

Really cute

Unbelievably cute

Too cute! How can you stand it?

Cutest thing I did today: _____

_____

Trouble scale

Who me?

Why can't we play fetch in the house?

Shoes are delicious

Coming up with a plan

Little angel

Trouble I got into: _____

_____

It was ◯ fun ◯ really fun

My walk(s)

Where: _____

What I saw / smelled: _____

Things I peed on: _____ Squirrel! ◯ Y ◯ N

Good things that happened today

- ◯ Play catch
- ◯ Chew toy
- ◯ Car ride
- ◯ Brushed
- ◯ Belly rub
- ◯ Scratch behind the ears
- ◯ Nap

Food: _____

Treat: _____

Playtime: _____

Other: _____

If I had thumbs I would: _____
_____
_____
_____

Lesson my owner learned from me today: _____
_____
_____
_____

Thought for the day: _____
_____
_____
_____

Draw what I am thinking right now:

Dogs are lousy poker players. When they get a good hand they wag their tails.
—AUTHOR UNKNOWN

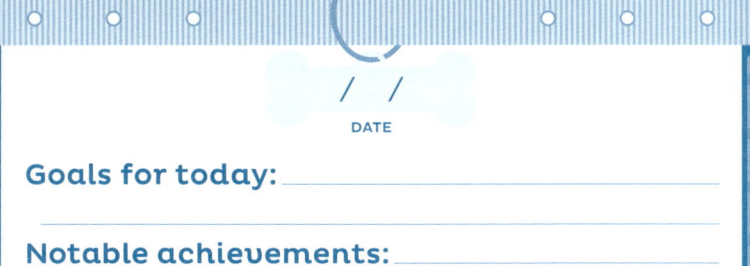

/ /

DATE

Goals for today: _____

_____

Notable achievements: _____

_____ Who's a good boy / girl? ◯ I am!

Cuteness scale

Cute

So cute

Really cute

Unbelievably cute

Too cute! How can you stand it?

Cutest thing I did today: _____

_____

Trouble scale

Who me?

Why can't we play fetch in the house?

Shoes are delicious

Coming up with a plan

Little angel

Trouble I got into: _____

_____

It was ◯ fun ◯ really fun

My walk(s)

Where: _____

What I saw / smelled: _____

Things I peed on: _____ Squirrel! ◯ Y ◯ N

Good things that happened today

- ◯ Play catch
- ◯ Chew toy
- ◯ Car ride
- ◯ Brushed
- ◯ Belly rub
- ◯ Scratch behind the ears
- ◯ Nap

Food: _____

Treat: _____

Playtime: _____

Other: _____

If I had thumbs I would: _____

Lesson my owner learned from me today: _____

Thought for the day: _____

Draw what I am thinking right now:

Outside of a dog, a book is man's best friend. Inside a dog, it's too dark to read.
—GROUCHO MARX

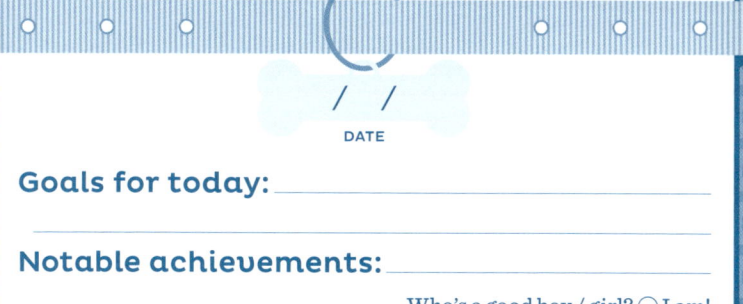

/ /

DATE

Goals for today: _____

_____

Notable achievements: _____

_____ Who's a good boy / girl? ◯ I am!

Cuteness scale

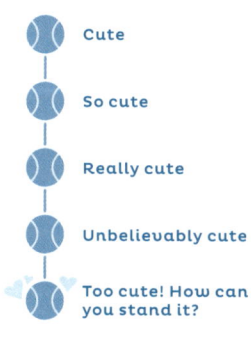

Cute

So cute

Really cute

Unbelievably cute

Too cute! How can you stand it?

Cutest thing I did today: _____

_____

Trouble scale

Who me?

Why can't we play fetch in the house?

Shoes are delicious

Coming up with a plan

Little angel

Trouble I got into: _____

_____

It was ◯ fun ◯ really fun

My walk(s)

Where: _____

What I saw / smelled: _____

Things I peed on: _____ Squirrel! ◯ Y ◯ N

Good things that happened today

- ◯ Play catch
- ◯ Chew toy
- ◯ Car ride
- ◯ Brushed
- ◯ Belly rub
- ◯ Scratch behind the ears
- ◯ Nap

Food: _____

Treat: _____

Playtime: _____

Other: _____

If I had thumbs I would: _____

Lesson my owner learned from me today: _____

Thought for the day: _____

Draw what I am thinking right now:

Dogs lead a nice life. You never see a dog with a wristwatch.
—GEORGE CARLIN

/ /

DATE

Goals for today: _____

_____

Notable achievements: _____

_____ Who's a good boy / girl? ◯ I am!

Cuteness scale

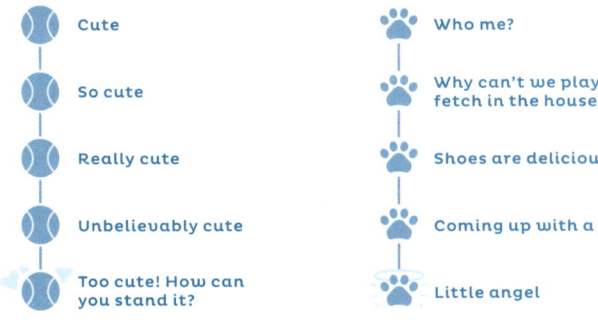

Cute

So cute

Really cute

Unbelievably cute

Too cute! How can you stand it?

Trouble scale

Who me?

Why can't we play fetch in the house?

Shoes are delicious

Coming up with a plan

Little angel

Cutest thing I did today: _____

_____

Trouble I got into: _____

It was ◯ fun ◯ really fun

My walk(s)

Where: _____

What I saw / smelled: _____

Things I peed on: _____ Squirrel! ◯ Y ◯ N

Good things that happened today

- ○ Play catch
- ○ Chew toy
- ○ Car ride
- ○ Brushed
- ○ Belly rub
- ○ Scratch behind the ears
- ○ Nap

Food: _____

Treat: _____

Playtime: _____

Other: _____

If I had thumbs I would: _____
_____
_____
_____

Lesson my owner learned from me today: _____
_____
_____
_____

Thought for the day: _____
_____
_____
_____

Draw what I am thinking right now:

The great pleasure of a dog is that you may make a fool of yourself with him and not only will he not scold you, but he will make a fool of himself, too.
—SAMUEL BUTLER

/ /

DATE

Goals for today: _____

_____

Notable achievements: _____

_____ Who's a good boy / girl? ◯ I am!

Cuteness scale

Cute

So cute

Really cute

Unbelievably cute

Too cute! How can you stand it?

Cutest thing I did today: _____

_____

Trouble scale

Who me?

Why can't we play fetch in the house?

Shoes are delicious

Coming up with a plan

Little angel

Trouble I got into: _____

_____

It was ◯ fun ◯ really fun

My walk(s)

Where: _____

What I saw / smelled: _____

Things I peed on: _____ Squirrel! ◯ Y ◯ N

Good things that happened today

- ◯ Play catch
- ◯ Chew toy
- ◯ Car ride
- ◯ Brushed
- ◯ Belly rub
- ◯ Scratch behind the ears
- ◯ Nap

Food: _____

Treat: _____

Playtime: _____

Other: _____

If I had thumbs I would: _____

Lesson my owner learned from me today: _____

Thought for the day: _____

Draw what I am thinking right now:

Dogs are my favorite people.
—RICHARD DEAN ANDERSON

/ / /
DATE

Goals for today: _____

_____

Notable achievements: _____

_____ Who's a good boy / girl? ◯ I am!

Cuteness scale

● Cute

● So cute

● Really cute

● Unbelievably cute

● Too cute! How can you stand it?

Cutest thing I did today: _____

_____

Trouble scale

Who me?

Why can't we play fetch in the house?

Shoes are delicious

Coming up with a plan

Little angel

Trouble I got into: _____

_____

It was ◯ fun ◯ really fun

My walk(s)

Where: _____

What I saw / smelled: _____

Things I peed on: _____ Squirrel! ◯ Y ◯ N

Good things that happened today

- ○ Play catch
- ○ Chew toy
- ○ Car ride
- ○ Brushed
- ○ Belly rub
- ○ Scratch behind the ears
- ○ Nap

Food: _____

Treat: _____

Playtime: _____

Other: _____

If I had thumbs I would: _____

Lesson my owner learned from me today: _____

Thought for the day: _____

Draw what I am thinking right now:

A dog is the only thing on earth that loves you more than he loves himself.
—JOSH BILLINGS

/ /

DATE

Goals for today: _____

_____

Notable achievements: _____

_____ Who's a good boy / girl? ○ I am!

Cuteness scale

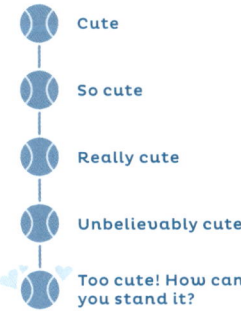

Cute

So cute

Really cute

Unbelievably cute

Too cute! How can you stand it?

Cutest thing I did today: _____

_____

Trouble scale

Who me?

Why can't we play fetch in the house?

Shoes are delicious

Coming up with a plan

Little angel

Trouble I got into: _____

_____

It was ○ fun ○ really fun

My walk(s)

Where: _____

What I saw / smelled: _____

Things I peed on: _____ Squirrel! ○ Y ○ N

Good things that happened today

- ○ Play catch
- ○ Chew toy
- ○ Car ride
- ○ Brushed
- ○ Belly rub
- ○ Scratch behind the ears
- ○ Nap

Food: _____

Treat: _____

Playtime: _____

Other: _____

If I had thumbs I would: _____

Lesson my owner learned from me today: _____

Thought for the day: _____

Draw what I am thinking right now:

If it wasn't for dogs, some people would never go for a walk.
—AUTHOR UNKNOWN

DATE

Goals for today: _____
_____

Notable achievements: _____
_____ Who's a good boy / girl? ◯ I am!

Cuteness scale

Cute

So cute

Really cute

Unbelievably cute

Too cute! How can you stand it?

Trouble scale

Who me?

Why can't we play fetch in the house?

Shoes are delicious

Coming up with a plan

Little angel

Cutest thing I did today: _____
_____

Trouble I got into: _____
_____

It was ◯ fun ◯ really fun

My walk(s)

Where: _____

What I saw / smelled: _____

Things I peed on: _____ Squirrel! ◯ Y ◯ N

Good things that happened today

- ◯ Play catch
- ◯ Chew toy
- ◯ Car ride
- ◯ Brushed
- ◯ Belly rub
- ◯ Scratch behind the ears
- ◯ Nap

Food: _____

Treat: _____

Playtime: _____

Other: _____

Draw what I am thinking right now:

If I had thumbs I would: _____

Lesson my owner learned from me today: _____

Thought for the day: _____

There is no psychiatrist in the world like a puppy licking your face.

—BEN WILLIAMS

/ /

DATE

Goals for today: _____

_____

Notable achievements: _____

_____ Who's a good boy / girl? ○ I am!

Cuteness scale

Cute

So cute

Really cute

Unbelievably cute

Too cute! How can you stand it?

Cutest thing I did today: _____

_____

Trouble scale

Who me?

Why can't we play fetch in the house?

Shoes are delicious

Coming up with a plan

Little angel

Trouble I got into: _____

It was ○ fun ○ really fun

My walk(s)

Where: _____

What I saw / smelled: _____

Things I peed on: _____ Squirrel! ○ Y ○ N

Good things that happened today

- ◯ Play catch
- ◯ Chew toy
- ◯ Car ride
- ◯ Brushed
- ◯ Belly rub
- ◯ Scratch behind the ears
- ◯ Nap

Food: _____

Treat: _____

Playtime: _____

Other: _____

Draw what I am thinking right now:

If I had thumbs I would: _____
_____
_____
_____

Lesson my owner learned from me today: _____
_____
_____
_____

Thought for the day: _____
_____
_____
_____

Dogs are lousy poker players. When they get a good hand they wag their tails.
—AUTHOR UNKNOWN

/ /
DATE

Goals for today: _____

_____

Notable achievements: _____

_____ Who's a good boy / girl? ⃝ I am!

Cuteness scale

🎾 Cute

🎾 So cute

🎾 Really cute

🎾 Unbelievably cute

🎾 Too cute! How can you stand it?

Cutest thing I did today: _____

_____

Trouble scale

🐾 Who me?

🐾 Why can't we play fetch in the house?

🐾 Shoes are delicious

🐾 Coming up with a plan

🐾 Little angel

Trouble I got into: _____

_____

It was ⃝ fun ⃝ really fun

My walk(s)

Where: _____

What I saw / smelled: _____

Things I peed on: _____ Squirrel! ⃝ Y ⃝ N

Good things that happened today

- ○ Play catch
- ○ Chew toy
- ○ Car ride
- ○ Brushed
- ○ Belly rub
- ○ Scratch behind the ears
- ○ Nap

Food: _____

Treat: _____

Playtime: _____

Other: _____

If I had thumbs I would: _____

Lesson my owner learned from me today: _____

Thought for the day: _____

Draw what I am thinking right now:

Outside of a dog, a book is man's best friend. Inside a dog, it's too dark to read.
—GROUCHO MARX

/ /
DATE

Goals for today: _____

_____

Notable achievements: _____

_____ Who's a good boy / girl? ○ I am!

Cuteness scale

Cute

So cute

Really cute

Unbelievably cute

Too cute! How can you stand it?

Trouble scale

Who me?

Why can't we play fetch in the house?

Shoes are delicious

Coming up with a plan

Little angel

Cutest thing I did today: _____

_____

Trouble I got into: _____

_____

It was ○ fun ○ really fun

My walk(s)

Where: _____

What I saw / smelled: _____

Things I peed on: _____ Squirrel! ○ Y ○ N

Good things that happened today

- ◯ Play catch
- ◯ Chew toy
- ◯ Car ride
- ◯ Brushed
- ◯ Belly rub
- ◯ Scratch behind the ears
- ◯ Nap

Food: _____

Treat: _____

Playtime: _____

Other: _____

If I had thumbs I would: _____

Lesson my owner learned from me today: _____

Thought for the day: _____

Draw what I am thinking right now:

Dogs lead a nice life. You never see a dog with a wristwatch.
—GEORGE CARLIN

_/ _/

DATE

Goals for today: _____

_____

Notable achievements: _____

_____ Who's a good boy / girl? ◯ I am!

Cuteness scale

Cute

So cute

Really cute

Unbelievably cute

Too cute! How can you stand it?

Cutest thing I did today: _____

_____

Trouble scale

Who me?

Why can't we play fetch in the house?

Shoes are delicious

Coming up with a plan

Little angel

Trouble I got into: _____

_____

It was ◯ fun ◯ really fun

My walk(s)

Where: _____

What I saw / smelled: _____

Things I peed on: _____ Squirrel! ◯ Y ◯ N

Good things that happened today

- ○ Play catch
- ○ Chew toy
- ○ Car ride
- ○ Brushed
- ○ Belly rub
- ○ Scratch behind the ears
- ○ Nap

Food: _____

Treat: _____

Playtime: _____

Other: _____

If I had thumbs I would: _____
_____
_____
_____

Lesson my owner learned from me today: _____
_____
_____
_____

Thought for the day: _____
_____
_____
_____

Draw what I am thinking right now:

The great pleasure of a dog is that you may make a fool of yourself with him and not only will he not scold you, but he will make a fool of himself, too.

—SAMUEL BUTLER

/ /

DATE

Goals for today: _____

_____

Notable achievements: _____

_____ Who's a good boy / girl? ○ I am!

Cuteness scale

- Cute
- So cute
- Really cute
- Unbelievably cute
- Too cute! How can you stand it?

Cutest thing I did today: _____

_____

Trouble scale

- Who me?
- Why can't we play fetch in the house?
- Shoes are delicious
- Coming up with a plan
- Little angel

Trouble I got into: _____

_____

It was ○ fun ○ really fun

My walk(s)

Where: _____

What I saw / smelled: _____

Things I peed on: _____ Squirrel! ○ Y ○ N

Good things that happened today

- ◯ Play catch
- ◯ Chew toy
- ◯ Car ride
- ◯ Brushed
- ◯ Belly rub
- ◯ Scratch behind the ears
- ◯ Nap

Food: _____

Treat: _____

Playtime: _____

Other: _____

If I had thumbs I would: _____
_____
_____
_____

Lesson my owner learned from me today: _____
_____
_____
_____

Thought for the day: _____
_____
_____
_____

Draw what I am thinking right now:

Dogs are my favorite people.
—RICHARD DEAN ANDERSON

/ /
DATE

Goals for today: _____

_____

Notable achievements: _____

_____ Who's a good boy / girl? ○ I am!

Cuteness scale

Cute

So cute

Really cute

Unbelievably cute

Too cute! How can you stand it?

Trouble scale

Who me?

Why can't we play fetch in the house?

Shoes are delicious

Coming up with a plan

Little angel

Cutest thing I did today: _____

_____

Trouble I got into: _____

_____

It was ○ fun ○ really fun

My walk(s)

Where: _____

What I saw / smelled: _____

Things I peed on: _____ Squirrel! ○ Y ○ N

Good things that happened today

- ○ Play catch
- ○ Chew toy
- ○ Car ride
- ○ Brushed
- ○ Belly rub
- ○ Scratch behind the ears
- ○ Nap

Food: _____

Treat: _____

Playtime: _____

Other: _____

If I had thumbs I would: _____

Lesson my owner learned from me today: _____

Thought for the day: _____

Draw what I am thinking right now:

A dog is the only thing on earth that loves you more than he loves himself.
—JOSH BILLINGS

/ /

DATE

Goals for today: _____

_____

Notable achievements: _____

_____ Who's a good boy / girl? ◯ I am!

Cuteness scale

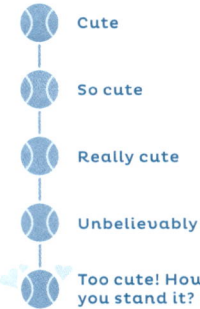

Cute

So cute

Really cute

Unbelievably cute

Too cute! How can you stand it?

Trouble scale

Who me?

Why can't we play fetch in the house?

Shoes are delicious

Coming up with a plan

Little angel

Cutest thing I did today: _____

_____

Trouble I got into: _____

_____

It was ◯ fun ◯ really fun

My walk(s)

Where: _____

What I saw / smelled: _____

Things I peed on: _____ Squirrel! ◯ Y ◯ N

Good things that happened today

- ◯ Play catch
- ◯ Chew toy
- ◯ Car ride
- ◯ Brushed
- ◯ Belly rub
- ◯ Scratch behind the ears
- ◯ Nap

Food: _____

Treat: _____

Playtime: _____

Other: _____

If I had thumbs I would: _____

Lesson my owner learned from me today: _____

Thought for the day: _____

Draw what I am thinking right now:

If it wasn't for dogs, some people would never go for a walk.
—AUTHOR UNKNOWN

/ /
DATE

Goals for today: _____

_____

Notable achievements: _____

_____ Who's a good boy / girl? ◯ I am!

Cuteness scale

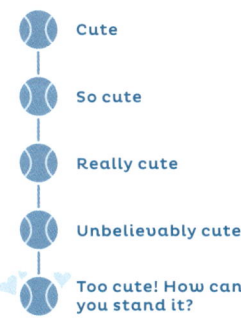

Cute

So cute

Really cute

Unbelievably cute

Too cute! How can you stand it?

Cutest thing I did today: _____

_____

Trouble scale

Who me?

Why can't we play fetch in the house?

Shoes are delicious

Coming up with a plan

Little angel

Trouble I got into: _____

_____

It was ◯ fun ◯ really fun

My walk(s)

Where: _____

What I saw / smelled: _____

Things I peed on: _____ Squirrel! ◯ Y ◯ N

Good things that happened today

- ○ Play catch
- ○ Chew toy
- ○ Car ride
- ○ Brushed
- ○ Belly rub
- ○ Scratch behind the ears
- ○ Nap

Food: _____

Treat: _____

Playtime: _____

Other: _____

If I had thumbs I would: _____

Lesson my owner learned from me today: _____

Thought for the day: _____

Draw what I am thinking right now:

There is no psychiatrist in the world like a puppy licking your face.
—BEN WILLIAMS

/ /

DATE

Goals for today: _____

_____

Notable achievements: _____

_____ Who's a good boy / girl? ◯ I am!

Cuteness scale

🎾 Cute

🎾 So cute

🎾 Really cute

🎾 Unbelievably cute

🎾 Too cute! How can you stand it?

Cutest thing I did today: _____

_____

My walk(s)

Where: _____

What I saw / smelled: _____

Things I peed on: _____

Trouble scale

🐾 Who me?

🐾 Why can't we play fetch in the house?

🐾 Shoes are delicious

🐾 Coming up with a plan

🐾 Little angel

Trouble I got into: _____

It was ◯ fun ◯ really fun

Squirrel! ◯ Y ◯ N

Good things that happened today

- ○ Play catch
- ○ Chew toy
- ○ Car ride
- ○ Brushed
- ○ Belly rub
- ○ Scratch behind the ears
- ○ Nap

Food: _____

Treat: _____

Playtime: _____

Other: _____

If I had thumbs I would: _____

Lesson my owner learned from me today: _____

Thought for the day: _____

Draw what I am thinking right now:

Dogs are lousy poker players. When they get a good hand they wag their tails.
—AUTHOR UNKNOWN

DATE

Goals for today: _____

_____

Notable achievements: _____

_____ Who's a good boy / girl? ◯ I am!

Cuteness scale

Cute

So cute

Really cute

Unbelievably cute

Too cute! How can you stand it?

Trouble scale

Who me?

Why can't we play fetch in the house?

Shoes are delicious

Coming up with a plan

Little angel

Cutest thing I did today: _____

_____

Trouble I got into: _____

_____

It was ◯ fun ◯ really fun

My walk(s)

Where: _____

What I saw / smelled: _____

Things I peed on: _____ Squirrel! ◯ Y ◯ N

Good things that happened today

- ◯ Play catch
- ◯ Chew toy
- ◯ Car ride
- ◯ Brushed
- ◯ Belly rub
- ◯ Scratch behind the ears
- ◯ Nap

Food: _____
Treat: _____
Playtime: _____
Other: _____

Draw what I am thinking right now:

If I had thumbs I would: _____

Lesson my owner learned from me today: _____

Thought for the day: _____

Outside of a dog, a book is man's best friend. Inside a dog, it's too dark to read.
—GROUCHO MARX

/ /

DATE

Goals for today: _____

_____

Notable achievements: _____

_____ Who's a good boy / girl? ◯ I am!

Cuteness scale

Cute

So cute

Really cute

Unbelievably cute

Too cute! How can you stand it?

Cutest thing I did today: _____

_____

Trouble scale

Who me?

Why can't we play fetch in the house?

Shoes are delicious

Coming up with a plan

Little angel

Trouble I got into: _____

_____

It was ◯ fun ◯ really fun

My walk(s)

Where: _____

What I saw / smelled: _____

Things I peed on: _____ Squirrel! ◯ Y ◯ N

Good things that happened today

- ○ Play catch
- ○ Chew toy
- ○ Car ride
- ○ Brushed
- ○ Belly rub
- ○ Scratch behind the ears
- ○ Nap

Food: _____

Treat: _____

Playtime: _____

Other: _____

If I had thumbs I would: _____

Lesson my owner learned from me today: _____

Thought for the day: _____

Draw what I am thinking right now:

Dogs lead a nice life. You never see a dog with a wristwatch.
—GEORGE CARLIN

/ /
DATE

Goals for today: _____

_____

Notable achievements: _____

_____ Who's a good boy / girl? ○ I am!

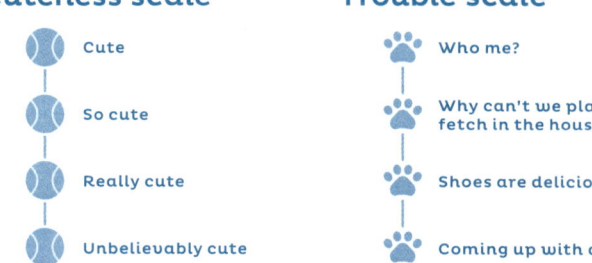

Cuteness scale

Cute

So cute

Really cute

Unbelievably cute

Too cute! How can you stand it?

Trouble scale

Who me?

Why can't we play fetch in the house?

Shoes are delicious

Coming up with a plan

Little angel

Cutest thing I did today: _____

_____

Trouble I got into: _____

_____

It was ○ fun ○ really fun

My walk(s)

Where: _____

What I saw / smelled: _____

Things I peed on: _____ Squirrel! ○ Y ○ N

Good things that happened today

- ◯ Play catch
- ◯ Chew toy
- ◯ Car ride
- ◯ Brushed
- ◯ Belly rub
- ◯ Scratch behind the ears
- ◯ Nap

Food: _____

Treat: _____

Playtime: _____

Other: _____

If I had thumbs I would: _____

Lesson my owner learned from me today: _____

Thought for the day: _____

Draw what I am thinking right now:

The great pleasure of a dog is that you may make a fool of yourself with him and not only will he not scold you, but he will make a fool of himself, too.

—SAMUEL BUTLER

/ /

DATE

Goals for today: _____

_____

Notable achievements: _____

_____ Who's a good boy / girl? ◯ I am!

Cuteness scale

Cute

So cute

Really cute

Unbelievably cute

Too cute! How can you stand it?

Cutest thing I did today: _____

_____

Trouble scale

Who me?

Why can't we play fetch in the house?

Shoes are delicious

Coming up with a plan

Little angel

Trouble I got into: _____

_____

It was ◯ fun ◯ really fun

My walk(s)

Where: _____

What I saw / smelled: _____

Things I peed on: _____ Squirrel! ◯ Y ◯ N

Good things that happened today

- ◯ Play catch
- ◯ Chew toy
- ◯ Car ride
- ◯ Brushed
- ◯ Belly rub
- ◯ Scratch behind the ears
- ◯ Nap

Food: _____

Treat: _____

Playtime: _____

Other: _____

If I had thumbs I would: _____
_____
_____
_____

Lesson my owner learned from me today: _____
_____
_____
_____

Thought for the day: _____
_____
_____

Draw what I am thinking right now:

Dogs are my favorite people.
—RICHARD DEAN ANDERSON

/ /

DATE

Goals for today: _____

_____

Notable achievements: _____

_____ Who's a good boy / girl? ○ I am!

Cuteness scale

● Cute

● So cute

● Really cute

● Unbelievably cute

● Too cute! How can you stand it?

Cutest thing I did today: _____

_____

Trouble scale

🐾 Who me?

🐾 Why can't we play fetch in the house?

🐾 Shoes are delicious

🐾 Coming up with a plan

🐾 Little angel

Trouble I got into: _____

_____

It was ○ fun ○ really fun

My walk(s)

Where: _____

What I saw / smelled: _____

Things I peed on: _____ Squirrel! ○ Y ○ N

Good things that happened today

- ○ Play catch
- ○ Chew toy
- ○ Car ride
- ○ Brushed
- ○ Belly rub
- ○ Scratch behind the ears
- ○ Nap

Food: _____

Treat: _____

Playtime: _____

Other: _____

If I had thumbs I would: _____

Lesson my owner learned from me today: _____

Thought for the day: _____

Draw what I am thinking right now:

A dog is the only thing on earth that loves you more than he loves himself.
—JOSH BILLINGS

/ /

DATE

Goals for today: _____

_____

Notable achievements: _____

_____ Who's a good boy / girl? ○ I am!

Cuteness scale

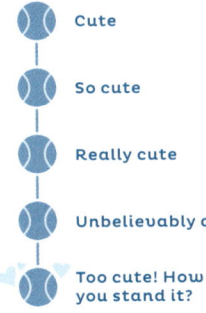

Cute

So cute

Really cute

Unbelievably cute

Too cute! How can
you stand it?

Cutest thing I did today: _____

_____

Trouble scale

Who me?

Why can't we play
fetch in the house?

Shoes are delicious

Coming up with a plan

Little angel

Trouble I got into: _____

It was ○ fun ○ really fun

My walk(s)

Where: _____

What I saw / smelled: _____

Things I peed on: _____ Squirrel! ○ Y ○ N

Good things that happened today

- ◯ Play catch
- ◯ Chew toy
- ◯ Car ride
- ◯ Brushed
- ◯ Belly rub
- ◯ Scratch behind the ears
- ◯ Nap

Food: _____

Treat: _____

Playtime: _____

Other: _____

If I had thumbs I would: _____

Lesson my owner learned from me today: _____

Thought for the day: _____

Draw what I am thinking right now:

If it wasn't for dogs, some people would never go for a walk.
—AUTHOR UNKNOWN

/ /

DATE

Goals for today: _____

_____

Notable achievements: _____

_____ Who's a good boy / girl? ○ I am!

Cuteness scale

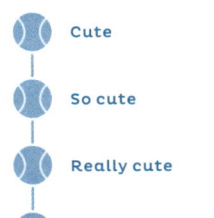

Cute

So cute

Really cute

Unbelievably cute

Too cute! How can you stand it?

Cutest thing I did today: _____

_____

Trouble scale

Who me?

Why can't we play fetch in the house?

Shoes are delicious

Coming up with a plan

Little angel

Trouble I got into: _____

_____

It was ○ fun ○ really fun

My walk(s)

Where: _____

What I saw / smelled: _____

Things I peed on: _____ Squirrel! ○ Y ○ N

Good things that happened today

- ○ Play catch
- ○ Chew toy
- ○ Car ride
- ○ Brushed
- ○ Belly rub
- ○ Scratch behind the ears
- ○ Nap

Food: _____

Treat: _____

Playtime: _____

Other: _____

Draw what I am thinking right now:

If I had thumbs I would: _____

Lesson my owner learned from me today: _____

Thought for the day: _____

There is no psychiatrist in the world like a puppy licking your face.

—BEN WILLIAMS

/ /

DATE

Goals for today: _____

_____

Notable achievements: _____

_____ Who's a good boy / girl? ○ I am!

Cuteness scale

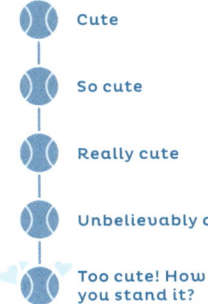

Cute

So cute

Really cute

Unbelievably cute

Too cute! How can you stand it?

Cutest thing I did today: _____

_____

Trouble scale

Who me?

Why can't we play fetch in the house?

Shoes are delicious

Coming up with a plan

Little angel

Trouble I got into: _____

It was ○ fun ○ really fun

My walk(s)

Where: _____

What I saw / smelled: _____

Things I peed on: _____ Squirrel! ○ Y ○ N

Good things that happened today

- ◯ Play catch
- ◯ Chew toy
- ◯ Car ride
- ◯ Brushed
- ◯ Belly rub
- ◯ Scratch behind the ears
- ◯ Nap

Food: _____

Treat: _____

Playtime: _____

Other: _____

If I had thumbs I would: _____

Lesson my owner learned from me today: _____

Thought for the day: _____

Draw what I am thinking right now:

Dogs are lousy poker players. When they get a good hand they wag their tails.

—AUTHOR UNKNOWN

_ / / _
DATE

Goals for today: _____
_____

Notable achievements: _____
_____ Who's a good boy / girl? ◯ I am!

Cuteness scale

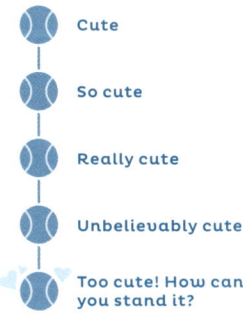

Cute

So cute

Really cute

Unbelievably cute

Too cute! How can you stand it?

Cutest thing I did today: _____
_____

Trouble scale

Who me?

Why can't we play fetch in the house?

Shoes are delicious

Coming up with a plan

Little angel

Trouble I got into: _____
_____

It was ◯ fun ◯ really fun

My walk(s)

Where: _____

What I saw / smelled: _____

Things I peed on: _____ Squirrel! ◯ Y ◯ N

Good things that happened today

- ◯ Play catch
- ◯ Chew toy
- ◯ Car ride
- ◯ Brushed
- ◯ Belly rub
- ◯ Scratch behind the ears
- ◯ Nap

Food: _____

Treat: _____

Playtime: _____

Other: _____

If I had thumbs I would: _____

Lesson my owner learned from me today: _____

Thought for the day: _____

Draw what I am thinking right now:

Outside of a dog, a book is man's best friend. Inside a dog, it's too dark to read.
—GROUCHO MARX

/ /
DATE

Goals for today: _____

_____

Notable achievements: _____

_____ Who's a good boy / girl? ◯ I am!

Cuteness scale

Cute

So cute

Really cute

Unbelievably cute

Too cute! How can you stand it?

Cutest thing I did today: _____

_____

Trouble scale

Who me?

Why can't we play fetch in the house?

Shoes are delicious

Coming up with a plan

Little angel

Trouble I got into: _____

_____

It was ◯ fun ◯ really fun

My walk(s)

Where: _____

What I saw / smelled: _____

Things I peed on: _____ Squirrel! ◯ Y ◯ N

Good things that happened today

- ○ Play catch
- ○ Chew toy
- ○ Car ride
- ○ Brushed
- ○ Belly rub
- ○ Scratch behind the ears
- ○ Nap

Food: _____

Treat: _____

Playtime: _____

Other: _____

If I had thumbs I would: _____

Lesson my owner learned from me today: _____

Thought for the day: _____

Draw what I am thinking right now:

Dogs lead a nice life. You never see a dog with a wristwatch.
—GEORGE CARLIN

/ /
DATE

Goals for today: _____

_____

Notable achievements: _____

_____ Who's a good boy / girl? ◯ I am!

Cuteness scale

◉ Cute

◉ So cute

◉ Really cute

◉ Unbelievably cute

◉ Too cute! How can you stand it?

Cutest thing I did today: _____

_____

Trouble scale

🐾 Who me?

🐾 Why can't we play fetch in the house?

🐾 Shoes are delicious

🐾 Coming up with a plan

🐾 Little angel

Trouble I got into: _____

_____

It was ◯ fun ◯ really fun

My walk(s)

Where: _____

What I saw / smelled: _____

Things I peed on: _____ Squirrel! ◯ Y ◯ N

Good things that happened today

- ⭘ Play catch
- ⭘ Chew toy
- ⭘ Car ride
- ⭘ Brushed
- ⭘ Belly rub
- ⭘ Scratch behind the ears
- ⭘ Nap

Food: _____

Treat: _____

Playtime: _____

Other: _____

If I had thumbs I would: _____

Lesson my owner learned from me today: _____

Thought for the day: _____

Draw what I am thinking right now:

The great pleasure of a dog is that you may make a fool of yourself with him and not only will he not scold you, but he will make a fool of himself, too.

—SAMUEL BUTLER

/ /

DATE

Goals for today: _____

_____

Notable achievements: _____

_____ Who's a good boy / girl? ◯ I am!

Cuteness scale

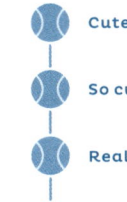 Cute

So cute

Really cute

Unbelievably cute

 Too cute! How can you stand it?

Cutest thing I did today: _____

_____

Trouble scale

 Who me?

Why can't we play fetch in the house?

Shoes are delicious

Coming up with a plan

Little angel

Trouble I got into: _____

_____

It was ◯ fun ◯ really fun

My walk(s)

Where: _____

What I saw / smelled: _____

Things I peed on: _____ Squirrel! ◯ Y ◯ N

Good things that happened today

- ◯ Play catch
- ◯ Chew toy
- ◯ Car ride
- ◯ Brushed
- ◯ Belly rub
- ◯ Scratch behind the ears
- ◯ Nap

Food: _____

Treat: _____

Playtime: _____

Other: _____

If I had thumbs I would: _____

Lesson my owner learned from me today: _____

Thought for the day: _____

Draw what I am thinking right now:

Dogs are my favorite people.
—RICHARD DEAN ANDERSON

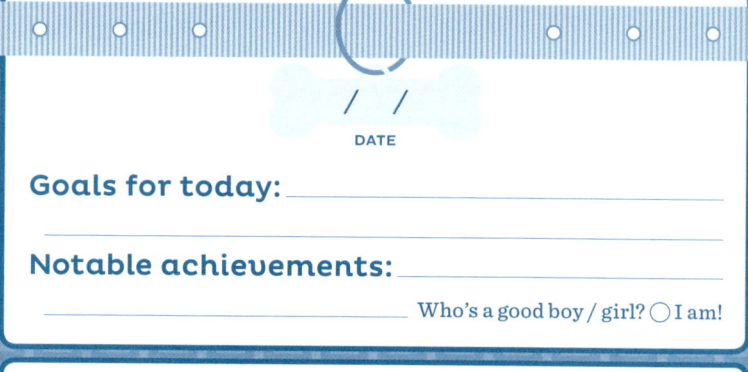

DATE / /

Goals for today: _____

_____

Notable achievements: _____

_____ Who's a good boy / girl? ◯ I am!

Cuteness scale

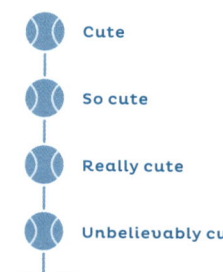

Cute

So cute

Really cute

Unbelievably cute

Too cute! How can you stand it?

Cutest thing I did today: _____

_____

Trouble scale

Who me?

Why can't we play fetch in the house?

Shoes are delicious

Coming up with a plan

Little angel

Trouble I got into: _____

_____

It was ◯ fun ◯ really fun

My walk(s)

Where: _____

What I saw / smelled: _____

Things I peed on: _____ Squirrel! ◯ Y ◯ N

Good things that happened today

- ○ Play catch
- ○ Chew toy
- ○ Car ride
- ○ Brushed
- ○ Belly rub
- ○ Scratch behind the ears
- ○ Nap

Food: _____

Treat: _____

Playtime: _____

Other: _____

If I had thumbs I would: _____

Lesson my owner learned from me today: _____

Thought for the day: _____

Draw what I am thinking right now:

A dog is the only thing on earth that loves you more than he loves himself.
—JOSH BILLINGS

/ /

DATE

Goals for today: _____

_____

Notable achievements: _____

_____ Who's a good boy / girl? ◯ I am!

Cuteness scale

- Cute
- So cute
- Really cute
- Unbelievably cute
- Too cute! How can you stand it?

Cutest thing I did today: _____

_____

My walk(s)

Where: _____

What I saw / smelled: _____

Things I peed on: _____

Trouble scale

- Who me?
- Why can't we play fetch in the house?
- Shoes are delicious
- Coming up with a plan
- Little angel

Trouble I got into: _____

_____

It was ◯ fun ◯ really fun

Squirrel! ◯ Y ◯ N

Good things that happened today

- ◯ Play catch
- ◯ Chew toy
- ◯ Car ride
- ◯ Brushed
- ◯ Belly rub
- ◯ Scratch behind the ears
- ◯ Nap

Food: _____

Treat: _____

Playtime: _____

Other: _____

If I had thumbs I would: _____

Lesson my owner learned from me today: _____

Thought for the day: _____

Draw what I am thinking right now:

If it wasn't for dogs, some people would never go for a walk.
—AUTHOR UNKNOWN